behind
the
changes

THE MUSIC OF RON CARTER

behind the changes

contents

A Letter From Ron Carter

Dear fellow bassists, men and women! In 2016 I was rehearsing in a freezing cold room with tenor saxophonist Javon Jackson and drummer Billy Drummond. We all had to get our fingers warmed up for a while before we could record. When we got a few choruses in, Billy asked me

"How do you do that?"

I thought he meant how do I warm up my fingers so quickly and I started to answer him. "No, no" he said "How do you do THAT" I thought a bit more and then started to answer about my hand position. Again, he said, "NO! When we got to the second chorus

you did all new changes.

HOW DO YOU DO THAT?!"
I was a bit taken aback, since that was something I have always done intuitively without thinking about it. I told him I needed time to be able to put it into words someone else would understand.

That was the beginning of a two-year process in my teaching that culminated in the publication of this book, whose main purpose is to

free musicians up to explore options.

Anyone, at any level can do this, as long as you have played the tune as written a long time.

After that, you can start to experiment on your own with it and get creative. My personal musical quest has always been "finding the right notes" I hope this book helps you find your right notes, that it inspires you and shows you how to explore options, take more harmonic risks, and make your own music for a lifetime.

Ron Carter

How to Use This Book

Leaf through this book and you will find pages with the original chords to a song (my tune "Saguaro", or song form (rhythm changes, 12 bar blues changes.) These represent three very common types of tunes that everyone plays.

The interesting part is on the pages with the red chords superimposed on the original chords. These contain various changes that I created myself. And there are more than one so each chorus can have a whole new set of harmonic changes.

These give you some examples of what you can do. These were my choices, but they are certainly not the only ones.

Keep looking back and forth between the basic changes and the new ones and see what different choices you might make.

There are QR codes throughout, that link to play-along tracks for each of the basic changes, the featured variations, and your own changes you can write after studying this book.

Charlie Parker changed the melody. We're not doing that. We are going to change the changes.

The Big Transcription Myth

I hear all the time from students who ask me which bass lines are most worth transcribing. I always have the same answer. "Don't waste time transcribing, it won't teach you how to do what they did."

Here's why: The beautiful tune that would be a transcription-worthy event was actually a happy accident that occurred on the spot and under perfect conditions. That bass line was something that was developing in real time as the musicians played.

The bassist made a harmonic choice in his or her bass line and the group picked up on it and developed it. In doing so the bassist took a risk – that the rest of the band would like it, and be able to run with it and develop it themselves. For example Herbie Hancock "heard" the chords which my bass lines implied and played them instantly.

Transcription-worthy performances are the result of a perfect storm occurring as the band plays together. There was no winning formula anyone could use to reproduce the same event under different conditions with different players. So the musician who transcribes it has no more of a clue of how to create that in the first place, than they did when they just listened and appreciated it... unless he or she has a plan or method that allows him or her to create interesting and possible "transcription-worthy" bass lines, chorus after chorus.

That's the core of this book

How you can make your own roadmap to changing the changes. You will see examples of harmonic variations (alternate changes) using common song forms (3) to show you just how these substitute chords look against the backdrop of the original chord changes of these song forms.

I encourage you to think on your own which notes to play, and not to just play the given changes. Spend time studying this book and you will gradually gain confidence in taking risks in making your own great harmonic choices that will inspire and lift your band to music that others want to transcribe.

5 Puzzle-Pieces to Finding the Right Notes

Each note I play has these points of interest: Consider them all as you begin to experiment in finding the right notes:

PITCH:
Is it in tune?

SOUND:
How is the sound of that note?

LOCATION:
Where is that note located on the instruments and what notes are in that position?

HARMONIC VALUE:
What chord(s) does that note imply?

IS THIS THE BEST/RIGHT NOTE?
Don't forget the importance of how your new changes affect the melody!

Be Brave and Take Risks!

When playing live creatively, and making your own changes, there is always a risk.

For instance, maybe the soloist won't like what you choose. That's OK.
Try something else next time.

The way to make your own music "transcription worthy" is to:

1.
Unleash your creativity

2.
Put the time in for trial and error

3.
Practice, practice, practice!

Rhythm Changes

Rhythm Changes

Bb | Cm7 F7 | Dm7 G7 | Cm7 F7

1.

5 Bb Bb/D | Eb E° | Dm7 G7 | Cm7 F7

2.

9 Cm7 | F7 | Bb

11 D7 | | G7 |

15 C7 | | F7 |

19 Bb | Cm7 F7 | Dm7 G7 | Cm7 F7

23 Bb Bb/D | Eb E° | F/Bb F7 | Bb

Rhythm Changes

Dm	G⁷	Cm	F	D	Db⁷	C⁷	B⁷
Bb		Cm⁷	F⁷	Dm⁷	G⁷	Cm⁷	F⁷

(𝄢 4/4)

Bb		Eb	E°⁷	⌐1 Bb/F		F#m	B⁷
5 Bb	Bb/D	Eb	E°	Dm⁷	G⁷	Cm⁷	F⁷

⌐2 Bb/F			Bb⁷⁽b⁹⁾
9 Cm⁷	F⁷	Bb	

Am⁷		D⁷		Ebm	Ab	Dm⁷	G⁷
11 D⁷				G⁷			

C⁷	Db⁷	C⁷		F⁷		F⁷⁽♯⁵⁾	
15 C⁷				F⁷			

Bb	Bb⁷	C⁷	Db	D	Eb	E	F
19 Bb		Cm⁷	F⁷	Dm⁷	G⁷	Cm⁷	F⁷

E⁷	Eb⁷	D⁷	Db⁷	C⁷⁽b⁹⁾	F⁷⁽b⁵⁾	Bb⁷	
23 Bb	Bb/D	Eb	E°	F/Bb	F⁷	Bb	

Rhythm Changes

Bb   Cm⁷   F⁷   Dm⁷   G⁷   Cm⁷   F⁷

$\text{B}\flat \qquad \text{Cm}^7 \quad \text{F}^7 \qquad \text{Dm}^7 \quad \text{G}^7 \qquad \text{Cm}^7 \quad \text{F}^7$

1.

$5 \quad \text{B}\flat \quad \text{B}\flat/\text{D} \quad \text{E}\flat \quad \text{E}° \qquad \text{Dm}^7 \quad \text{G}^7 \qquad \text{Cm}^7 \quad \text{F}^7$

2.

$9 \quad \text{Cm}^7 \qquad \text{F}^7 \qquad \text{B}\flat$

$11 \quad \text{D}^7 \qquad \qquad \text{G}^7$

$15 \quad \text{C}^7 \qquad \qquad \text{F}^7$

$19 \quad \text{B}\flat \qquad \text{Cm}^7 \quad \text{F}^7 \qquad \text{Dm}^7 \quad \text{G}^7 \qquad \text{Cm}^7 \quad \text{F}^7$

$23 \quad \text{B}\flat \quad \text{B}\flat/\text{D} \quad \text{E}\flat \quad \text{E}° \qquad \text{F}/\text{B}\flat \quad \text{F}^7 \qquad \text{B}\flat$

Rhythm Changes

F#m   B^7 Em^7 A^7 D   D♭^{7} C^7 B^7
B♭   Cm^7 F^7 Dm^7 G^7 Cm^7 F^7

$\mathbf{9\!:}$ $\frac{4}{4}$

|1.
Bb   Eb   Ab   Db   Dm^7 Db^7 Cm^7 B^7
5 B♭   B♭/D   E♭   E°   Dm^7 G^7 Cm^7 F^7

|2.
Cm^7 F^7 A^7 B♭
9 Cm^7 F^7 B♭

A♭^{7} G^7
11 D^7 G^7

G♭^{7} C^7 F^7
15 C^7 F^7

B♭^{7} D♭^{7} E^7 F^7
19 B♭   Cm^7 F^7 Dm^7 G^7 Cm^7 F^7

Em^7 A^7 Dm^7 G^7 Cm^7 F^7 B♭   B^7
23 B♭   B♭/D   E♭   E°   F/B♭   F^7 B♭

12 Bar Blues

12 Bar Blues

F   B♭   F   F^7

5   B♭   B♭^{7} F   Dm

9   Gm   C^7 F   Dm   G^7 C^7

13   F   B♭   F   F^7

17   B♭   B♭^{7} F   Dm

21   Gm   C^7 F   Dm   G^7 C^7

12 Bar Blues

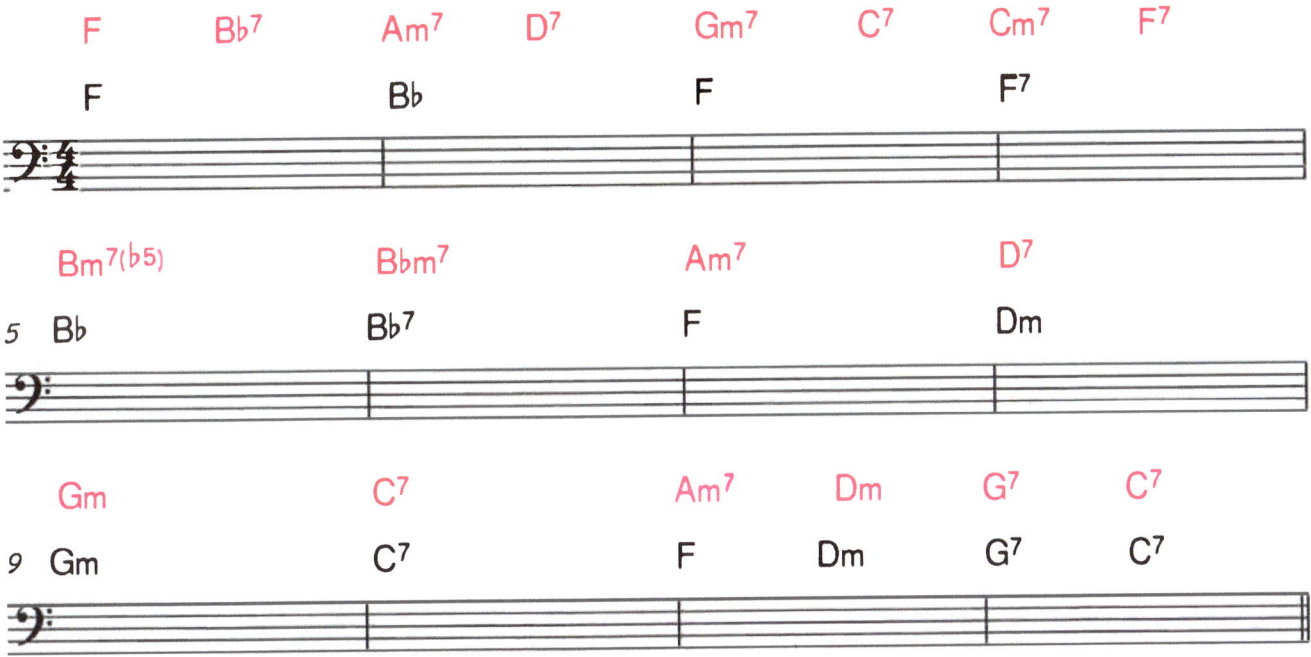

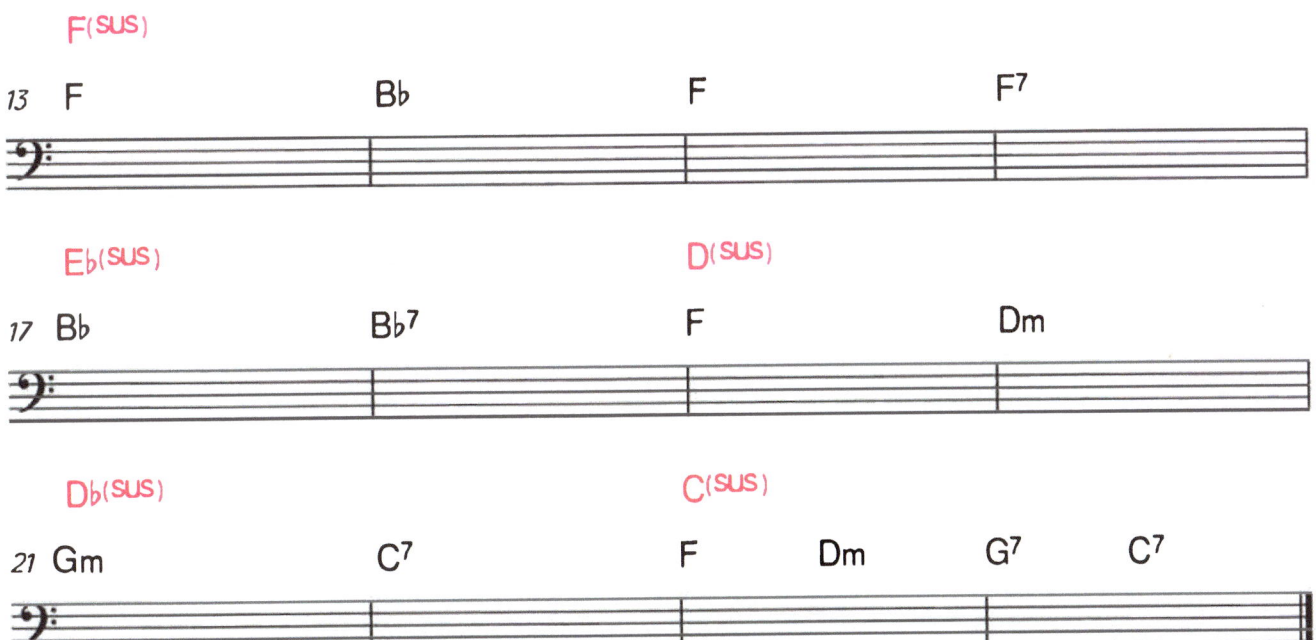

12 Bar Blues

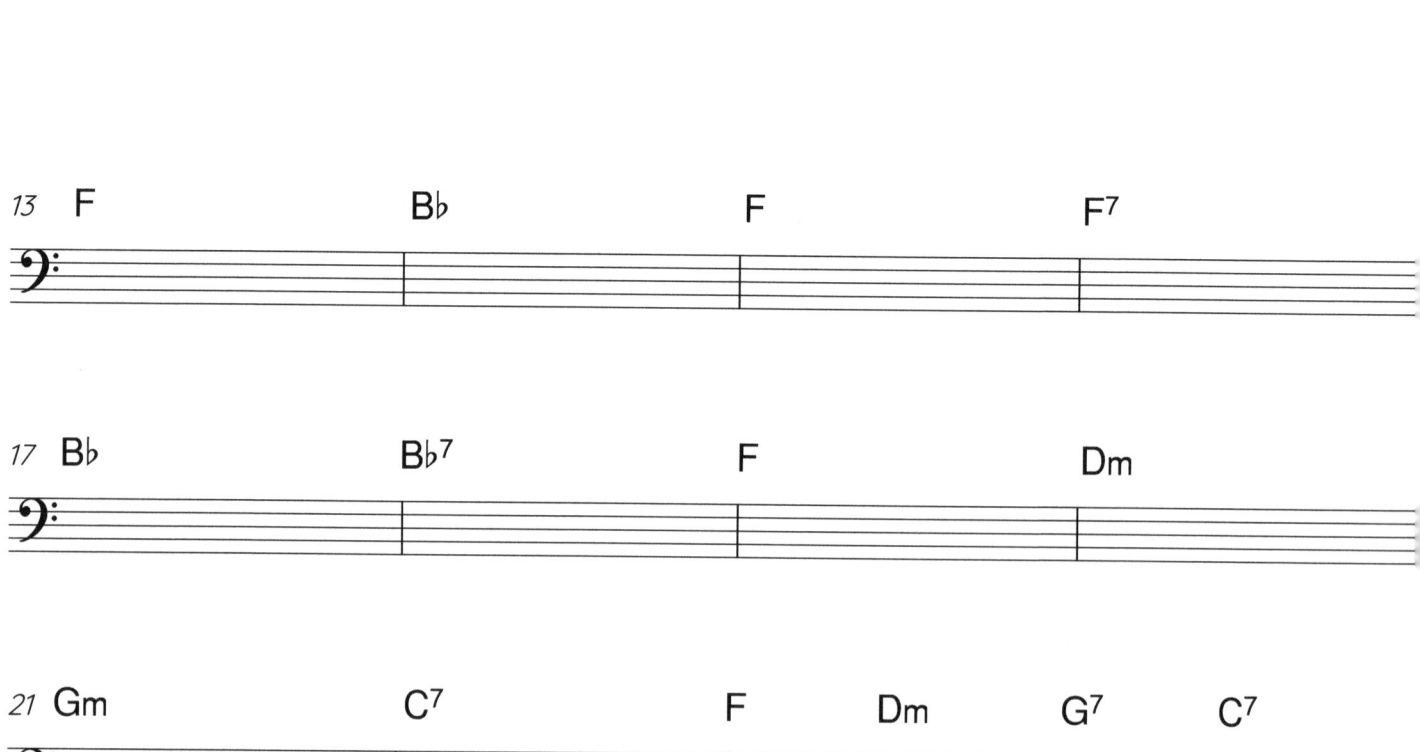

12 Bar Blues

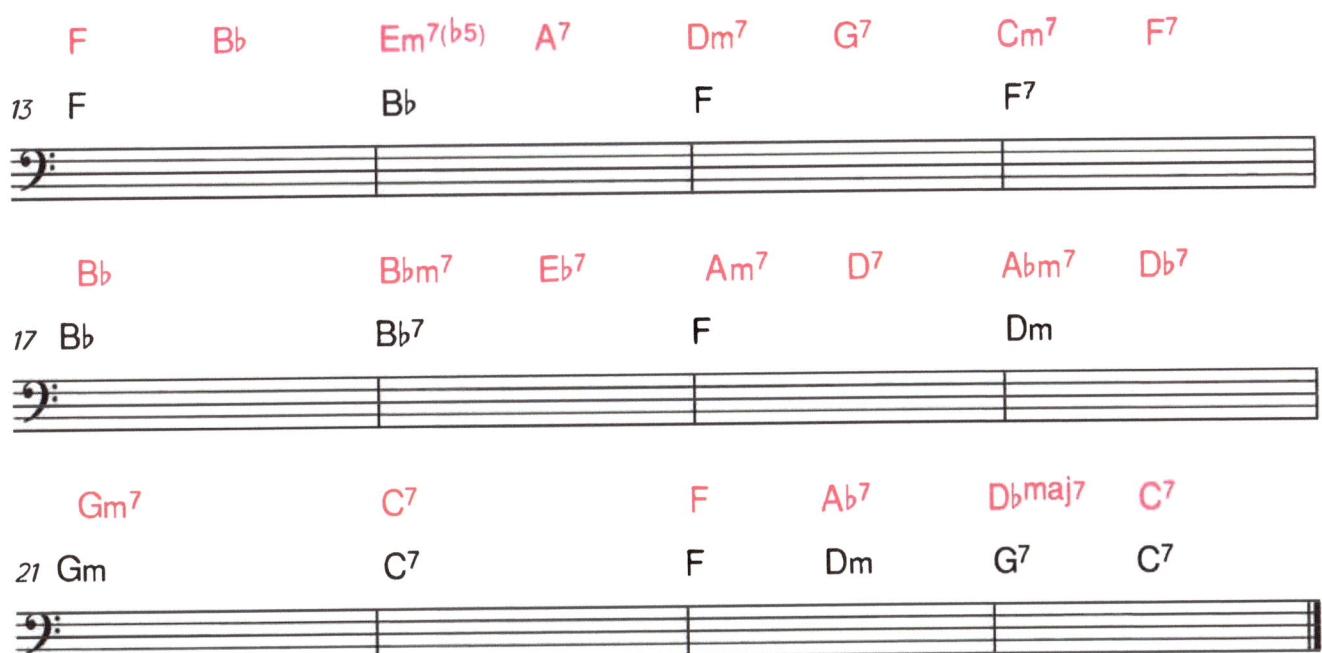

12 Bar Blues

| F | B♭ | F | F⁷ |

5 | B♭ | B♭⁷ | F | Dm |

9 | Gm | C⁷ | F | Dm | G⁷ | C⁷ |

13 | F | B♭ | F | F⁷ |

17 | B♭ | B♭⁷ | F | Dm |

21 | Gm | C⁷ | F | Dm | G⁷ | C⁷ |

12 Bar Blues

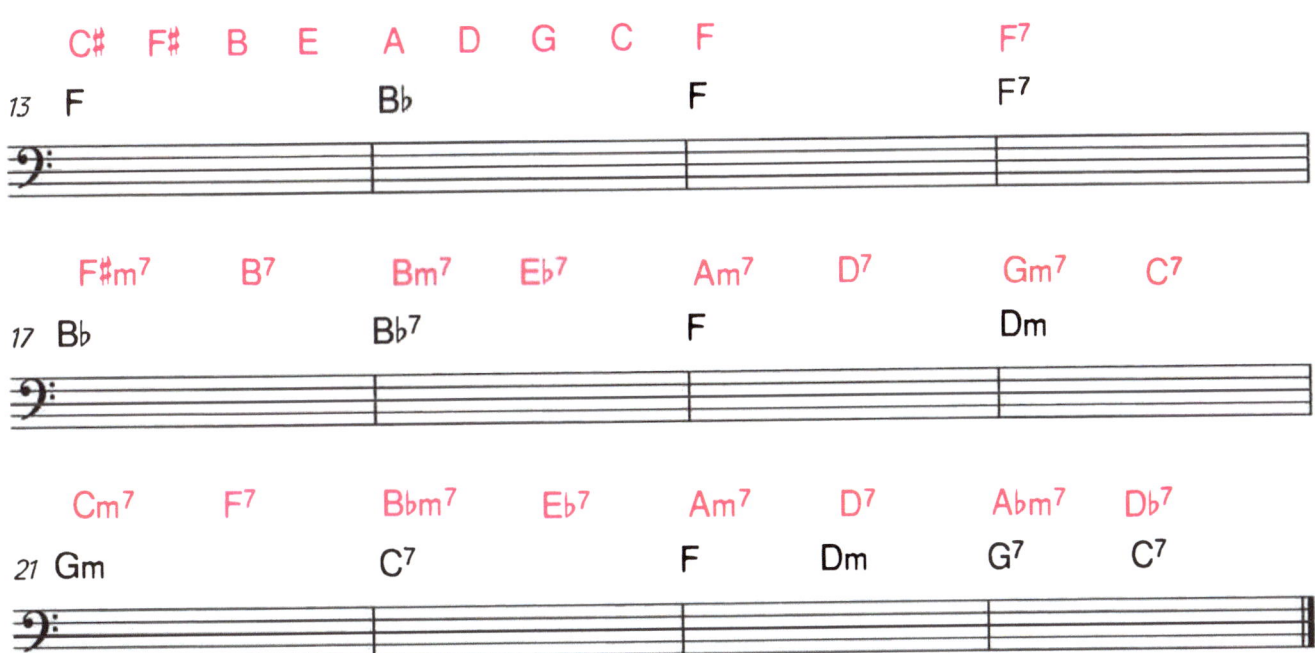

Sample Song
Saguaro

by Ron Carter

Saguaro

Ron Carter

| Cm⁷ | F⁷ | B♭maj7 | E♭maj7 |

$$\text{Cm}^7 \quad \text{F}^7 \quad \text{B}\flat\text{maj7} \quad \text{E}\flat\text{maj7}$$

5 $\text{Am}^{(\flat 5)}$ $\quad$ D^7 $\quad$ Gm

9 Cm^7 $\quad$ F^7 $\quad$ $\text{B}\flat\text{maj7}$ $\quad$ $\text{E}\flat\text{maj7}$

13 $\text{Am}^{(\flat 5)}$ $\quad$ D^7 $\quad$ Gm

17 D^7 $\quad$ Gm

21 Cm^7 $\quad$ F^7 $\quad$ $\text{B}\flat\text{maj7}$

25 $\text{Am}^{7(\flat 5)}$ $\quad$ D^7 $\quad$ Gm

29 $\text{Am}^{7(\flat 5)}$ $\quad$ D^7 $\quad$ Gm

Saguaro

Ron Carter

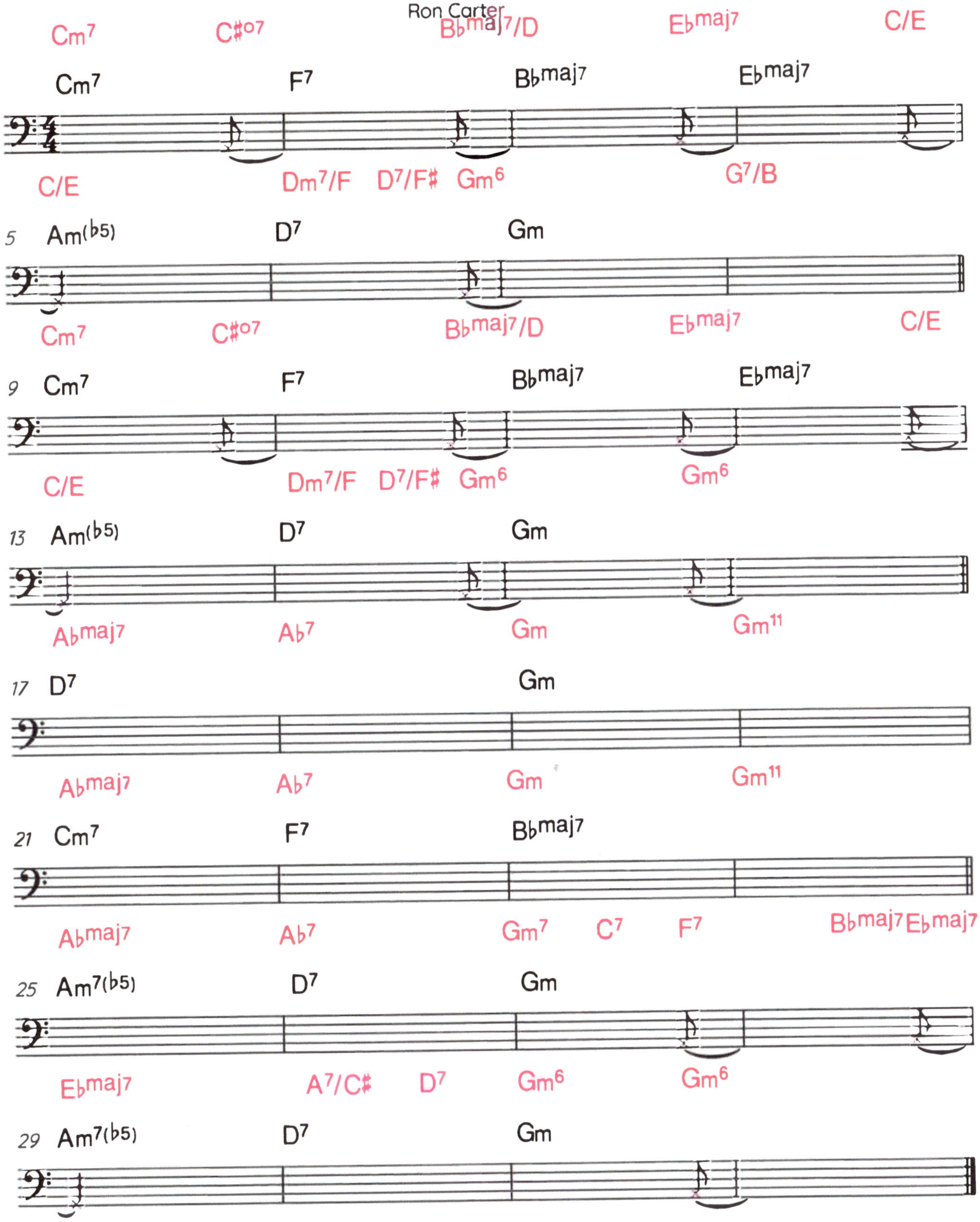

Cm⁷   C#º⁷   B♭maj7/D   E♭maj7   C/E

Cm⁷   F⁷   B♭maj7   E♭maj7

C/E   Dm⁷/F   D⁷/F#   Gm⁶   G⁷/B

5   Am⁽♭5⁾   D⁷   Gm

Cm⁷   C#º⁷   B♭maj7/D   E♭maj7   C/E

9   Cm⁷   F⁷   B♭maj7   E♭maj7

C/E   Dm⁷/F   D⁷/F#   Gm⁶   Gm⁶

13   Am⁽♭5⁾   D⁷   Gm

A♭maj7   A♭⁷   Gm   Gm¹¹

17   D⁷   Gm

A♭maj7   A♭⁷   Gm   Gm¹¹

21   Cm⁷   F⁷   B♭maj7

A♭maj7   A♭⁷   Gm⁷   C⁷   F⁷   B♭maj7   E♭maj7

25   Am⁷⁽♭5⁾   D⁷   Gm

E♭maj7   A⁷/C#   D⁷   Gm⁶   Gm⁶

29   Am⁷⁽♭5⁾   D⁷   Gm

Saguaro

Ron Carter

| Cm⁷ | F⁷ | B♭maj7 | E♭maj7 |

Line 1: **Cm^7** — **F^7** — **B$\flat$maj7** — **E$\flat$maj7**

5 **Am$^{(\flat5)}$** — **D^7** — **Gm**

9 **Cm^7** — **F^7** — **B$\flat$maj7** — **E$\flat$maj7**

13 **Am$^{(\flat5)}$** — **D^7** — **Gm**

17 **D^7** — **Gm**

21 **Cm^7** — **F^7** — **B$\flat$maj7**

25 **Am$^{7(\flat5)}$** — **D^7** — **Gm**

29 **Am$^{7(\flat5)}$** — **D^7** — **Gm**

Saguaro
Ron Carter

Cm⁷	F⁷/A	B♭/D	E♭/G
Cm⁷	F⁷	B♭maj7	E♭maj7

$\text{Cm}^7 \quad\quad \text{F}^7 \quad\quad \text{B}♭\text{maj7} \quad\quad \text{E}♭\text{maj7}$

(bass clef, 4/4)

Am⁷(♭5)		D⁷	A♭⁷(♯5)	Gm⁷

5   Am(♭5)   D⁷   Gm

Cm(maj7)/B	F/B♭ F⁷/A	B♭maj7	E♭maj7

9   Cm⁷   F⁷   B♭maj7   E♭maj7

Am⁷(♭5)	D⁷	B♭/A♭	B♭/A♭

13   Am(♭5)   D⁷   Gm

E♭maj7	E♭maj7	A♭⁷	A♭⁷

17   D⁷   Gm

A♭⁷	A♭⁷	Gm⁷	Gm⁷

21   Cm⁷   F⁷   B♭maj7

A♭⁷	A♭⁷	Gm⁷	Gm⁷

25   Am⁷(♭5)   D⁷   Gm

A♭⁷	A♭⁷	Gm⁷	G⁷/B

29   Am⁷(♭5)   D⁷   Gm

Saguaro

Ron Carter

Cm7 F7 B♭maj7 E♭maj7
5 Am(♭5) D7 Gm
9 Cm7 F7 B♭maj7 E♭maj7
13 Am(♭5) D7 Gm
17 D7 Gm
21 Cm7 F7 B♭maj7
25 Am7(♭5) D7 Gm
29 Am7(♭5) D7 Gm

Saguaro

Ron Carter

Em⁷	Ebm⁷	Bb/D	Db⁷
Cm⁷	F⁷	Bbmaj7	Ebmaj7

$\text{Em}^7 \quad \text{E}\flat\text{m}^7 \quad \text{B}\flat/\text{D} \quad \text{D}\flat^7$

$\text{Cm}^7 \quad \text{F}^7 \quad \text{B}\flat\text{maj7} \quad \text{E}\flat\text{maj7}$

5
Cm⁷	F⁷	Gm⁷	Gm⁷
Am(b5)	D⁷	Gm	

9
Em⁹(b5)	Ebm(maj7)	Bb(add2)/D	Db⁷
Cm⁷	F⁷	Bbmaj7	Ebmaj7

13
Gbmaj7	F⁷(sus)	Gm¹¹	Gm¹¹
Am(b5)	D⁷	Gm	

17
Ab⁷	B⁷ Bb⁷		Gm⁶
D⁷		Gm	

21
Ab⁷	D/F#	Gm⁶	Gm⁶
Cm⁷	F⁷	Bbmaj7	

25
Ab⁷	G⁷	Cm⁷ F⁷	Bbm⁷ Eb⁷
Am⁷(b5)	D⁷	Gm	

29
Ab⁷	Am⁷(b5) D⁷(b9)	Gm(maj7)	Gm(maj7)
Am⁷(b5)	D⁷	Gm	

Ab⁷

RON CARTER is among the most original, prolific and influential bassists in jazz. He has recorded over 2200 albums and has a Guinness World Record to prove it!

In Jazz: From 1963 to 1968 he was a member of the acclaimed Miles Davis Quintet. He can be heard on many iconic jazz records of the 60's and 70's such as Speak No Evil, Maiden Voyage, Red Clay, Speak Like a Child, Nefertiti and Miles Smiles, to name a few.

In other music genres: After leaving the quintet he embarked on a prolific 60-year free-lance career that spanned vastly different music genres and continues to this day. He recorded with Roberta Flack, Billy Joel, Bette Midler, Paul Simon and Aretha Franklin, appeared on the seminal hip-hop album Low End Theory with A Tribe Called Quest, wrote and recorded pieces for string quartets and Bach chorales for 2-6 bassists and accompanied Danny Simmons on a spoken word album.

As a leader: Carter continues to do worldwide tours with his various groups, The Foursight Quartet, The Golden Striker Trio, Ron Carter's Great Big Band and the Ron Carter Nonet. He has recorded multiple albums with his groups.

As an author: Carter shares his expertise in the series of books he has authored, in which he explains his creative process and teaches bassists to improve their skills and develop their own unique sound. His books share a unique feature he pioneered, that of including QR codes in every book that lead to additional material, enriching the text and making each book that much more valuable.

In 2015 he penned his autobiography "Finding the Right Notes" which is available in print and e-book and also as an audio book read by the Maestro himself.

In 2021 Carter pioneered a new type of music transcription with "Chartography", which follows the development of the bass line for Autumn Leaves over 5 performances with the Miles Davis Quintet, showing not only the bass line but also how the band responded to it and how the entire tune transformed over time.

As a teacher: Carter has lectured, conducted and performed at clinics and master classes, instructing jazz ensembles and teaching the business of music at numerous universities. He was Artistic Director of the Thelonious Monk Institute of Jazz Studies when it was located in Boston and after 18 years on the faculty of the Music Department of the City College of New York he is now Distinguished Professor Emeritus. He also taught at the Julliard School and and at Manhattan School of Music.

In film scoring: In addition to scoring and arranging music for many films, including some projects for the Public Broadcasting System, Carter composed music for "A Gathering of Old Men" starring Lou Gosset Jr., "The Passion of Beatrice" directed by Bertrand Tavernier, and "Blind Faith" starring Courtney B. Vance

Film Appearances: In October 2022 PBS released a full-length feature film documentary on the Maestro's life called Ron Carter: Finding the Right Notes. Many jazz documentaries feature the Maestro because of his indelible contribution to the genre including Ken Burns' "Jazz", "Birth of the Cool" about Miles Davis, "It Must Be Schwing", the story of the Blue Note and many more. He also appeared as himself in HBO's hit series "Treme" and was the bassist on the soundtrack of "Twin Peaks", "Bird" and way too many others to mention.

Awards:

Grammy Awards: In 2022 Carter won with "Skyline" for Best Instrumental Jazz Album. In 1993, he earned a Grammy award for Best Jazz Instrumental Group, the Miles Davis Tribute Band and another Grammy in 1998 for "Call Sheet Blues", an instrumental composition from the film, Round Midnight.

International Awards: In 2021 the Japanese government awarded him The Order of the Rising Sun, Gold Rays with Rosette for his contributions to Japan-US relations in the field of music. In 2021 Carter was honored by the French Minister of Culture with France's premier cultural award, the medallion and title of Commander of the Order of Arts and Letters, given to those who have distinguished themselves in the domain of artistic or literary creation and for their contribution to the spread of arts and letters in France and the world.

Guinness World Record: In 2015 Carter earned a Guinness World Record as the most recorded jazz bassist with 2,221 recordings. Since that time he has recorded hundreds more.

Press Awards: Ron Carter was named "Outstanding Bassist of the Decade" by the Detroit News, Jazz Bassist of the Year by Downbeat magazine, and Most Valuable Player by the National Academy of Recording Arts and Sciences several times.

Education Awards: Carter earned seven honorary doctorates, Manhattan School of Music (1998), from the New England Conservatory of Music (1999), Berklee (2005), University of Rochester (2010), University of Michigan, (2016), Juilliard (2018), Clark University 2023 and Yale (2025).

He was the 2002 recipient of the prestigious Hutchinson Award from the Eastman School at the University of Rochester

In 2021 he received the Satchmo Award from the Louis Armstrong Foundation for his lasting contribution to jazz as an educator.

THE COMPLETE RON CARTER LIBRARY

Transcriptions

Carter-isms: The Evolution of Bossa Nova Bass Lines from their origin in Brazil, to the New York Bossa sound that Carter created and continues to evolve today.

Chartography: Ron Carter's original, unique re-invention of transcriptions and their study. Transcriptions of the bass lines from 5 performances of Autumn Leaves by the Miles Davis Quintet. A detailed chart of how the bass line evolved and how the band responded. Includes QR codes to audio of each performance transcribed. Also available in Japanese.

The Art of Ron Carter 1963-1968 By Mikko Nurmi. Precise, accurate transcriptions of his bass lines and explanations of how and why they worked so well. 230 pages, a professional, literary presentation for all jazz bass historians and jazz bassists.

9 Transcriptions Every bassist should study

Books

Ron Carter: The Smithsonian Interview: Coffee table art book based on the full transcript of the historic 2011 interview for the Smithsonian Oral History Project.

Bass Drops: 30 Examples of Non-Quarter Note Bass Line Rhythms All Levels

Mix & Match: Advanced Guide to Creating Great Bass Lines. With "Dutch Door" pages to mix and match choruses and bass lines.

Comprehensive Bass Method Advanced Level: Shows bassists how to master pizzicato and horizontal technique. Also available in Japanese and Portuguese.

Behind the Changes: Intermediate guide to how to change the changes with each chorus. Transparent overlay pages Also available in Portuguese.

Blueprint for the Working Jazz Bassist: Intermediate guide to creating your own unique sound.

The Ron Carter Songbook: Includes Little Waltz, Eighty-One and 131 more Ron Carter compositions. Available in treble and bass clef.

Finding the Right Notes: Ron Carter's iconic autobiography. Available in paperback and e-book. Audio book, read by the Maestro himself.

From the Bottom Up: Creativity and Individuality in Jazz. Interviews with 7 legendary bassists. By Gui Duvigneau.

7 Unique Bass Arrangements: For solo performance and technical study by Dave Baron.

Scores and Parts

Scores and Parts for string ensembles: Arrangements of 4 Carter compositions:

2+1=4 for violin, viola and cello
Desert Winds and Loose Change each for 4 cellos
Serenade for viola and 4 cellos

Ron Carter Meets Bach: Scores and parts for 13 Bach chorales for 2-8 basses. Arranged by Ron Carter. Available in 3 volumes

Big Band Scores – 10 Ron Carter Compositions arranged by Rich DeRosa

Big Band Scores – 10 Jazz Standards plus 2 Ron Carter tunes arranged by Bob Freedman

Available at www.roncarterjazz.com and Amazon.com